Manifesto of American Dreamers

TOMISLAV BIRTIC

CONTENTS

The world is advancing because there are enough people who hope they will become so rich they will no longer have to work

1 THE SPECTRE OF THE AMERICAN DREAM AROUND THE WORLD

A spectre is going around the world. The spectre of the American dream.

All the powers of the world have got together in a holy alliance as the instigators of this spectre: Microsoft and the fighters against monopolies and crackers, Pepsi and Coca Cola, generals and pacifists, dictators and human rights' movements, Chevrolet and Honda and Mercedes, the oil industry and the Greens, the police and criminals, the left and right and the centre, the Pope and the patriarchs, believers and atheists, the fashion industry, feminists and housewives, the mass media and their audience and the intellectual elite...

If there is any party, whether in power or in opposition, who does not claim that precisely it is the progressive force which will equalize the conditions for success and literally give everyone the chance to realize their American dream? Where is there a successful person in any field of human activity who has not been declared the American dreamer?

Two things are true.

All the world powers agree that the American dream is a force in itself.

Alongside the law of supply and demand and capital, the American dream is the third pillar holding up civilization.

2 IN GOD WE TRUST. THE HELL WE DO!

History recalls several initiatives to create heaven on Earth. If religious books are to be believed, the first proposal was the work of God himself, but man rejected him, unreasonably, too lightly.

Man was given the ten commandments, the best constitution ever written, even better than the famous American one. One of the conditions for heaven on Earth was, "There shall be no other gods but me". Unfortunately, man did not understand that these were instructions for making use heaven, the advice of an experienced father who knows what life is and who tries to save his son from trouble, and not a command.

Rejecting God, man chose capital as his god, most often its most vulgar form, money, and the results were terrible.

The human race is divided into those who have and those who do not have the means of production, that is into capitalists and labourers.

The division by gender is unimportant, as is sexual orientation, skin colour, nation, religious affiliation...

Although in conflicts for which they were the cause, these differences resulted in impressive chunks of history, they do not form its backbone, possibly only its ribs.

Human history is apparently a story of the struggle of the immediate producers to capture the means of production.

For thousands of years the immediate producers thought that they would solve the problem of the fair distribution of wealth, and problems, in their opinion, (error!) occurred exclusively or primarily because of unfair distribution, if they acquired the means of production. Slave owner and slave, patrician and plebeian, feudal lord and serf, guild master and apprentice, bourgeois and proletarian, suppressor and suppressed stood against each other and fought each other, sometimes covertly sometimes overtly.

After thousands of years of indescribable inferiority, the immediate producer was finally in a position to rebel effectively and capture the means of production by force.

"Let the ruling classes tremble at a Communistic revolution. The proletarians have nothing to lose but their chains. They have a world to win," the communist threatened since the problem could not be resolved by dialogue. "Working Men of All Countries, Unite!"

Threatened and done. On the respectable area of the globe, the proletariat gained control of the means of production by force. He kidnapped them.

That is how communism came about, the minimalist and more humane variant of the American dream. Minimalist because instead of abundance it offered a bearable existence, more humane because instead of grandiose rewards for the most capable, most skilful or the luckiest minority, it prescribed a bearable life for all.

Man gained the opportunity for the cost of labour not to be determined by the superhuman and inhuman law of supply and demand, but for surplus value to be distributed fairly by human hands. Moreover, this was an opportunity, through care for children and the elderly, the health care system, humane housing conditions, and in general care for all those who could not care for themselves, for the price, the value of life to be determined by human will. For life to be what it is, priceless.

We gained the dictator-proletarian, who failed the test of expertise and humanity. Having captured the means of production, that is the entire world, the proletarian did not know what to do with them. Able to wield a club, skilled in shooting and screwing screws or threshing grain, the communist proved to be incapable of managing the means of production. He defended the position he had gained by annihilating all those who thought differently.

We also gained the ordinary proletarian, the greatest enemy of any completed revolution. Whilst the communist-dictator did business without a conscience, to the detriment of businesses, comfortably ensconced in the practice that notice was given with great difficulty or not at all, the ordinary communist proletarian, on a guaranteed minimum wage, by nature, dominated by idleness and petty thievery, undermined at all levels the order he had shed blood to win. He was the greatest hindrance to prosperity and all the other precious goals of the noble idea of communism.

Communism depended too much on man, that is, his good will to be human, to do all he could to be called human. Capitalism survived and continues to survive, because it does not depend on man; this dominant social order contains in itself a mechanism which guards man successfully from human nature, from "humanity".

In contrast to communism, which can survive, and survival means progress, only if a critical mass has a very, very high level of consciousness, for the progress of capitalism no consciousness is necessary at all. Or, the only consciousness that is needed in capitalism is that you have to respect the simple rule of pleasing the customer; if you are the owner of a company, in order to avoid bankruptcy, or if you are only the immediate producer, to avoid being fired. Simply, natural selection.

However irresponsible a worker is, with supervision (capitalism has refined Lenin's idea to perfection that a man is better when he is controlled, and Stalin's idea that love is transient, but only fear is eternal) and in fear of being fired, he simply cannot be lazy and irresponsible, and as such, he is protected from himself, so produces and in the end, earns sufficiently to be content. Or at least he has a greater chance of being more productive than the competition and earns enough to be satisfied. Household appliances have made everyday life easier, and cinemas, television and baseball matches have revolutionized enjoyment. Capitalism fulfilled the workers' needs known as 888, or three times eight: eight hours of work, eight hours of rest and eight hours of cultural improvement. True, cultural improvement requires an effort and workers need relaxation, so they fill the eight hours planned for cultural improvement with entertainment, but with the addition of mandatory annual leave, we have the ideal picture. Presented with these benefits, the hired worker thanked God that he had never inherited communism, and his eastern neighbour, looking at such abundance, came to hate his eight hours of idleness, eight hours of drivel about cultural improvement, cursed the bad television program and the lack of money to go to the seaside, and his eight hours of unearned rest.

Actually the fact was that for mankind as a species, for the animal who worked hard in capitalism and who was idle in communism, a bearable existence was not sufficient. The experiment of communism proved that history is not the story of the efforts of those who do not own the means of production to acquire them and to distribute wealth fairly. After man gained the opportunity to determine his own fate, it turned out that the immediate producer was only saying that he wanted ownership of the means of production and justice, but in fact he wanted wealth, simply surplus value, money sufficient for his entire life, whereby it was not at all important where that money came from. It is an undisputed fact that the true name of that desire is to get so rich that you do not have to work for the rest of your life, or so you can work as much as you want and when you want. Communism, or let's call it socialism, helped by loans from capitalist countries, was only a bastard derivative, a derivative of the desire for enormous wealth.

Communism, above all, collapsed because a few, the management of the epoch, realized the American dream, it collapsed because the American dream was not realized on the market, but first of all by revolution and then (single party) elections, whilst American dreaming for most was strictly forbidden and declared counter-revolutionary; the prohibition of American dreaming, it is true, was compensated for by the corruption of the masses, whereby whilst communism did not consume its own substance it was permissible to do practically nothing. The bearable existence of the masses relieved of competition for jobs quickly collapsed into the unbearable, the number of crimes committed by general secretaries grew to the unbearable, as did the poverty of their subjects, and the children of the revolution sought forgiveness from capital; wars or less fierce conflicts occurred on the territories were people were convinced that someone had stolen from them the chance to realize the American dream, and it is necessary to notice that communism came about because American dreaming was forbidden, and collapsed because it forbade the American dream itself. The children of the revolution turned against communism with the same force their predecessors did against capitalism. With the same force and equally successfully, only with less casualties from bullets, and more from hunger, cold and other forms of poverty. The children of the revolution brought their sacrifices to capital, the general secretaries and their apostles.

But capital behaved like God in the Old Testament. The penalty for disrespect or ignorance of its law of supply and demand in countries where capitalism was introduced long ago is called bankruptcy, but it is cruel and merciless, even towards those innocent descendants of the arrogant sinners who dared to oppose its will, the law of supply and demand and the American dream. In states whose populations were bold enough to undertake a revolution and forbid American dreaming, capital's punishment is known as transition or colonization, most often by the taking of entire nations into slavery by means of loans, which any fool can see will never be returned.

We should in no way ignore the fact that the masses oscillate, public opinion first demands capitalism, then communism, then again capitalism, and in the end cries out for the humaner aspects of communism. This public opinion is only one of the key pieces of evidence that man does not accept, cannot accept, anything less than the American dream. However, if there was any doubt before the experiment called communism, if there was any justification for the misapprehension of the classes and the masses, after the experiment we have reached a conclusion. Communism is the key evidence that man cannot be reconciled to anything less than the realization of the American dream, with nothing less than words of indescribable wealth.

3 REVOLUTION, A SLIGHTLY MORE TEMPESTUOUS SHAREHOLDERS' ASSEMBLY THAN USUAL

Associations of citizens, or limited liability companies, whose listed or unlisted, formal or informal membership numbers millions or billions, strive for a goal so noble, that it is an insult to even call it super-party, let alone party, political, striving for citizens' association or a limited liability company to change the world for the better, to bring mankind as close to Utopia or the idyll as it is possible to be close to Utopia or the idyll, we could call that pursuit a movement.

There is no movement. Or, movement does not exist.

There is only capital and the law of supply and demand, with which from time immemorial human nature has reacted and correlated, equally. Only man, whether as an individual or as the collective consciousness, has wrongly interpreted this for many millennia.

It is untrue that the minority tried to suppress the majority by its decision. The minority did not decide anything, because it could not decide. No one was able to decide anything. It only appears to have always been a matter of getting more votes, the electoral process whereby the honest counting of votes is guaranteed by capital and the law of supply and demand. But, it is not man who decides, as the owner of capital, but the capital.

The statement: "All previous historical movements were movements of minorities, or in the interest of minorities. The proletarian movement is the self-conscious, independent movement of the immense majority, in the interest of the immense majority. The proletariat, the lowest stratum of our present society, cannot stir, cannot raise itself up, without the whole superincumbent strata of official society being sprung into the air," is, since Marx and Engels showed in other works that they understand the material, mere populism. The two of them understood how and why social orders are transformed. That is, not how one social order changes into another, when both are founded on capital, the law of supply and demand and the American dream, but capital, almost synonymous with consciousness, evolution, only perfects the same order. It perfects it into the only logical degree determined and governed by capital, the law of supply and demand and the American dream; human consciousness, whether collective or individual, according to Hegel the function of time, has nothing to do with it. So, the greatest sin of Marx and Engels is not the falsification of the past or the future, but the fact that they tabloidized the present they lived in. Exactly! The Communist Manifesto is a slimy text, humouring the masses like a tabloid, and nothing but spin. (The Manifesto of American Dreamers does not deal with other texts similar to the Communist Manifesto, but only with the Communist Manifesto, since in the history of mankind only communism has had a match point against capitalism, whilst all other Utopias, like sects created only for the needs of their gurus, have simply been outclassed.)

Rebellions by slaves were doomed to fail until production grew strong enough that the loss of the slaves, man reduced to the level of a tool, would mean a significant drop in production, a slowdown of progress. While there were more slaves than demand for them, their lives were almost worthless. With the growth of demand for their labour, the price of their labour also grew, as did their rights, and at the end of the process they became co-owners of the land, that is the means of production. By the same principle, feudalism was transformed into capitalism with the release of the serfs, and capitalism, with the arrival of the civil society, was refined into what we call capitalism with a human face, which capitalism certainly is not and never can have, since it is the nature of capitalism to trample down all in its path in the interests of progress.

So, the social order did not change by the decision of men, nor out of love, a moral crisis or blackmail, there was no thought process, but the changes were – paid for, they were the result of a growth in productivity, production, that is, the move of the increasing assets of the gross domestic product into the formula of capital, the law of supply and demand and the American dream.

In the sense, the context into which man was placed by Marx and Engels and many others, the so-called "ideologists", man does not exist. Man is simply an arm, a tool, practically a nerve ending of an ethereal being, the ethereal trinity of capital, the law of supply and demand and the American dream; man in the context of transformation of an order exists exactly as much as we can say that a billiard cue drives the balls into the holes and not the player. In the sense, the context we are talking about, man is just the cue, held in the hand of the triune god of capital, the law of supply and demand and the American dream.

Some ideologists were wrong, again and again, others consciously manipulated people with populism, overestimating man's role in history, claiming that societies have been transformed by revolutions. These so-called revolutions, violent changes of slave-ownership into feudalism, feudalism into capitalism, and capitalism into communism – were nothing more than common or garden shareholders' assemblies, albeit slightly more tempestuous than usual. Nothing other than a change in ownership structure. To put it simply, the one and only majority owner of a company decides alone and outvotes everyone else at the assembly. But in time, slavery, feudalism and capitalism were simply recapitalized by man and people, their share grew until they attained the majority needed to change the management of the epoch; we could call it a hostile takeover. Nothing other, both man and people are capital, the value of their share in the ownership structure of millennia or centuries of epochs grew enough for the management to be changed at the shareholders' assembly, and a new one installed. After the shareholders' assembly, the ideologists, the media before the media as we know it today, would be given such good positions, ranging from president of the state administration, or, if the ideologist wanted to have a little rest, he would be put in public relations or human resources.

It is only an illusion that "Hitherto, every form of society has been based, as we have already seen, on the antagonism of oppressing and oppressed classes. But in order to oppress a class, certain conditions must be assured to it under which it can, at least, continue its slavish existence." There are no classes, so there is no correlation between them. There is only a correlation between capital, the law of supply and demand and the American dream on the one hand, and the total outcome of production, surplus value expressed as capital, on the other. This relationship determined the fate of the members of the so-called classes; it is simply a matter of circumstances which turn carbon into diamonds or soot, or water into ice or steam.

Communism, the match point of mankind for which Man had struggled from time immemorial, even before the words communism and socialism were coined, but people did not make use of it, is a historical anomaly in territories with an excessively low gross domestic product, through the rebellion of the oppressed, not against the oppressors but against the ineffective use of capital, the law of supply and demand, and above all the American dream.

Not even the owners of the means of production, that is the owners of large capital, were above capital, the law of supply and demand and American dreaming. The clearest evidence that there is no lawlessness in that order are precisely the changes of the management of entire epochs.

4 IT'S NOT ENOUGH I TELL YOU!

Both the humanists and Marx and Engels overestimated man. Everyone from Jesus, through Marx and Engels, to John Lennon and the Beatles included the superman in the equation of the survival of communism or any form of Utopia, that is in the equation of their proposal to the shareholders for the appointment of new management, but actually what they were talking about was the little man.

Within capital, the law of supply and demand and American dreaming, there is no room for free will. That is, there is precisely as much as free will is aligned with the will of capital, the law of supply and demand and the American dream. There is as much free will in jumping out of aeroplanes as that free will is aligned with gravity and having or not having a parachute. Or, to put it more simply, the ideologists of the out-voted shareholders – dissatisfaction is a more precise word than oppression – made a bad mistake when they overlooked the fact that capital, the law of supply and demand and the American dream understand human nature and what man is made of much better, that is, the system of the triune god was created precisely in accordance with human nature.

Marx and Engels, as colleagues, poetically unjustifiably accused capitalism that, "It has drowned the most heavenly ecstasies of religious fervour, of chivalrous enthusiasm, of philistine sentimentalism, in the icy water of egotistical calculation", and that capitalism (a synonym for the bourgeoisie, actually a synonym for history until that time, that is, practice), "It has resolved personal worth into exchange value, and in place of the numberless indefeasible chartered freedoms, has set up that single, unconscionable freedom — Free Trade."

Simply, capital, the law of supply and demand and the American dream are aligned with human nature, in which Man, about whom Marx and Engels wrote the Communist Manifesto, and Man about whom religious books are written, and man or Man, about whom the song Imagine was written, is literally incidental. Religious fervour, chivalrous enthusiasm, philistine sentimentalism, personal worth are the higher levels of consciousness of the enlightened Man; the result of a higher level of consciousness, but in the love of man, demonstrated through donations and, for instance, the unburdened performances of sportsmen after they have attained freedom through realizing the American dream, we see that it is all about capital. Whilst religious fervour is aroused in people by – possession, especially of things bought with money they do not have to impress people they do not care about. A purely animal matter, but perfectly aligned with merciless capital, the law of supply and demand and the American dream, mostly the law of supply and demand, possession of other people's dignity is one of the more valuable status symbols (and often cheaper than a painting by Picasso, and certainly more widely available), as may be seen in human behaviour from earliest childhood, that is, from the time we begin to distinguish good and evil, right into deep old age, and also in the scale from indescribable poverty to the other extreme of wealth unimaginable for the human mind. The mere existence of possession of man or Man is abhorrent to Man, whilst amongst people possession literally proves their existence, and the peak of existence is possessing other people's dignity. This is nothing to do with capitalism, but with human nature, a constant of time.

Further, it is untrue that capitalism, "has stripped of its halo every occupation hitherto honoured and looked up to with reverent awe." Capitalism has not, "converted the physician, the lawyer, the priest, the poet, the man of science, into its paid wage labourers." There has always been respect for physicians, God's ambassadors on Earth, and always will be (in the trenches and hospitals everyone becomes a believer), and this respect has never minded in the least the fact that physicians, and all the others on the list of the respected, in all – not social orders but epochs – have always been paid wage labourers. However, capitalism in its development, the spread of surplus value from the classes to the masses, from the capitalist to the wage labourer, liberated the slave from dependence on the whim of the one and only monopolist or a few employers united in a duopoly or an oligopoly. Whether liberated from patrons or state dictatorship, however enlightened it was in some places, more blessed by the law of supply and demand than exposed to it, those employed in exalted professions attained the possibility of receiving a fair wage for their work. Of course that fair wage for work in public schools in ghettos is painfully low, whilst at Yale it is justifiably high. Concentrated on Man instead of on people, knowing everything about the law of supply and demand, Marx and Engels "overlooked" the correlation of the number of people interested in someone's product or service and the price of the work, which in the end a mindless girl with beautiful tits and ass, who in violence against the law of supply and demand would have no serious chance of earning in two hundred generations, does however had a chance in market competition to rise from an underdog to become the exalted desire not only of a doctor's dreams, but the dreams of millions or hundreds of millions of people; to be Pharaoh's chosen one means to be subject to his whim, whilst the exalted desire of the dreams of millions of people, easily finds a new buyer on the market of spirit and flesh. They did not overlook it, it was simply a good speech at the shareholders' assembly.

Also, capitalism has not, "torn away from the family its sentimental veil, and has reduced the family relation to a mere money relation." As in ordinary prostitution, refined prostitution is simply a historical constant amongst people, which, in the end was equally comfortable under communism. Again Man, and people...

If it were impossible to defend them with populism, excellent public relations, that is, spin, it would in fact be astounding how Marx and Engels only saw Man, and overlooked people. "Our bourgeois, not content with having wives and daughters of their proletarians at their disposal, not to speak of common prostitutes, take the greatest pleasure in seducing each other's wives."

If we only consider the majority owners of the means of production, a fan of Marx and Engels would defend his idols, saying that at that time there was no statistical sample of proletarian rulers, since neither the proletariat nor the proletarians had yet gained control of the means of production, that is, none of them had attained wealth, nor had they attained it as a collective. But, in the name of the law of supply and demand, capital and the American dream, seducing other people's wives had been known as long as monogamy; in polygamy it was still possible to make a mistake, but it is more difficult in monogamy. It was really unnecessary to be a prophet or a genius to know how Stalin, Tito or Mao would behave after they took control of the means of production, that is, after the assembly of shareholders set them up as the managing directors with unlimited authority. Just as it is well-known, however well we know that ladies choose, that success in seduction is proportional to capital. A whore is equal to a gigolo, but capital is always capital. Capital, whatever it is converted into, is always capital, in proletarian seduction of a proletarian's wife, or in a landowner's sex with his slave, or the Queen's decadent sport with a serf. Just as capital is always capital in the possession of an aircraft carrier in foreign affairs or a tank against demonstrators in so-called internal affairs, of course it is actually an internal or external shareholders' assembly; the victory of empty-handed demonstrators against tanks is mainly a matter of the support from powers with aircraft carriers. If we talk about size, and not about the negligible work of those capable of love, capital is the only stable factor of human relationships.

And, one of the worst insults of the Communist Manifesto against the natural order is the accusation that capitalism, "has disclosed how it came to pass that the brutal display of vigour... found its fitting complement in the most slothful indolence." The benefits of indolence are an insult to the classes, and even the masses feel offended, since, it is an indisputable truth, through its productiveness, capitalism revolutionised the indolence of the masses. Simply, indolence is a matter of simple surplus value, just as any entertainment is a matter of a surplus value, a matter of free time, the only non-renewable resource. From tourism to the evolution of pop from Mozart to rap, that is, the construction of the backbone of surplus value from the elite to the ghetto, it is nothing other than the revolution of the indolence of the masses.

The Communist Manifesto accuses capitalism, that it, "has through its exploitation of the world market given a cosmopolitan character to production and consumption in every country. To the great chagrin of Reactionists, it has drawn from under the feet of industry the national ground on which it stood." But capital, the law of supply and demand and the American dream succeeded where even religion did not: the holy trinity even directed people (not Man, who understands this, but billions of people) to respect true super-national values. Not Abraham Lincoln, Martin Luther, Nelson Mandela nor the Dalai Lama did harm to discrimination as much as the trinity of capital, the law of supply and demand and the American dream; simply, globalization powered by capital, the law of supply and demand and the American dream made narrow-mindedness unmarketable, bigoted ignoramuses ended up bankrupt or as mediocrities, and the holy trinity's mission of enlightenment moves inexorably on. So, if both religion and capital are to blame for a large amount of discrimination, if they have caused many conflicts, and it may be said that they have gathered an equal number of negative points through their atrocities, no religion alone nor all religions together can match capital in terms of its ecumenical effect. That is why we American dreamers consider accusations of the cosmopolitan character of the removal of national ground from under the feet of industry to be a compliment. We will continue to endeavour to wipe out the national boundaries between all human activities and create universal, universal everything, aligned with people and Man, but not the needs of the timid who, afraid of healthy competition, seek to pollute even the noblest human enterprise with customs duties, that is, to prevent progress by means of monopoly.

Communism did not succeed for the same reason religions have not succeeded, it came face to face with capital, the law of supply and demand and the American dream, that is, human nature. True, religions are slightly more successful than communism, since spiritual leadership does not also mean taking responsibility for the economic results of a group or an individual. However, they are not unsuccessful because all hungry people, choosing between a stone, wood or bread will choose bread, or because without external influences the result of the choice of religion would be a simple Gaussian function, but because religions are in conflict with human nature. This nature is brutally simple: man behaves well only towards those who increase his chance of survival, that is, he behaves well only towards those who increase his chances of progress.

Progress does not depend on man, but the holy trinity governs the evolution of human consciousness. Capital, the law of supply and demand and the American dream evolve what Hegel called consciousness, spirit, but we do stop at progress, since for the sake of progress even the development of consciousness can be halted. Indefinitely.

Capital, the law of supply and demand and the American dream, are the only natural order, that is the only order which is not an ideology, whilst all other proposals are actually nothing but mass therapy for unrealized American dreamers; let there be no mistake, these therapies can be quite lucrative.

It is clear that any abundance or over-abundance arises from want, since want is the best motivation, however, every time he overcomes want, man re-discovers indolence and forgets his duty to hand the world on to his descendants in a better state than what he found. Having won the struggle for an already very high standard of comfort, man, as a breed, began to complain about his life, which began to lose contact with nature and original human values, morals, ethics, and he increasingly began to visit psychiatrists, to turn to various religions and charlatans, and weaken himself as a productive force, able to give birth out in a field and continue to dig half an hour later.

The creator created a man who does nothing for free, a lazy bug who would not even reproduce his own kind if he were not rewarded by an orgasm, let alone continue through history without reward. Yes, in all epochs, like a baby given a pacifier to stop it crying, he needed to be kept happy to do works pleasing to God and capital.

For man to keep history alive, he was initially satisfied with bread and water, for a while he was happy with only conditional freedom, but when he began to see it as normal, even enriching it with free afternoons, annual leave, and elections without a property or at least an educational census, something new was needed. Specifically, man wanted to rule.

Developing the idea that nothing is free, or rather sliding down its slide, the law of supply and demand – in no way to escape from tyranny as a social order – began to enchant man once more: it made every consumer a king.

Indeed, as soon as you enter a store, as soon as you are the purchaser of goods or services, you automatically become the tip of a tiny pyramid – they kneel and beg you to return. Telling you you are the best – that your hair looks nice (they remember from last time), that it is a real shame you don't play basketball you are so tall (you would have all the money in the world) – they are more persuasive than a whore. This is not the normal courtesy learned from parents in the best families. Every time we buy something, it is true, only in countries where the initial accumulation came to an end at least thirty years ago, they act towards us exactly the way books describe the relationship between a subject and a king.

So, to have an entire kingdom you do not need to have even a noble title. Because your little money commands respect. When spending, even the tradesman's smile is enough of a kingdom for you to feel dignity, absolutely sufficient in your bearable existence for you to kneel with a smile before the purchaser of your product.

In developed capitalism man is not only king as consumer, but also as a common worker. To protect the growth of production, capital ordered the owners of means of production to improve the conditions of work. So owners of factories send their employees for further training, buy them protective clothing, in many companies they even worry about the colour of the walls, not to mention the lighting of the working environment.

But even that is not enough. The stability of the system is constantly being threatened by insecurity and monotony.

All are rulers and all are slaves, both the owners of the means of production and their employees. The market changes too quickly for all our tastes, destinies collapse in a second with the failure of a business or an entire branch of industry. Or the stock markets. The vast majority feel insecure, and fear is proportional to age.

Freedom is the number of days we can survive without any form of income. From hunters and gatherers, through slaves and serfs, to hired workers, the average duration of personal peace has increased. Surplus value is sufficient for one day, a week, a month, a year, ten years...

It is not enough! There is a strong desire rooted in man for surplus value which will guarantee him the satisfaction of all his needs for his entire life, and eternal insecurity is the generator of the American dream almost as much as monotony.

In contrast to slaves and serfs, who were constantly under armed supervision, frustrated civilians may at first sight leave behind the boring production process at any time, but in fact they are tame, helpless as animals in a zoo. Man, trapped in the triangle of his house, work and the pub, can become a danger to his environment, and if enough of them get together, to capital too. In order for him not to go crazy from monotony, like a dropper, the American dream helps him, the illusion that he will be rescued from his cage.

From the time of slavery, when the American dream was realized by birth or the whim of the king, right up to capitalism, no one has talked about the American dream as the final and only desire, the super-religion, the only religion which unites the human race ecumenically, simply because productivity or its synonym, the gross national product per head of the population, is not sufficient for capital and the law of supply and demand to produce a sufficient number of satisfied American dreamers within a unit of time for the American dream to be institutionalized as a religion.

But, clearly, due to the stability it gives the system, the American dream is one of the most important products of capital and the law of supply and demand.

Therefore it is indisputable that the American dream is a key factor in the future development of civilization.

The progress of the human race is nothing but a side-effect of American dreaming.

If the number of American dreamers were to fall below a critical level, either we would kill each other off, or someone would occupy the masses with some form of revolution, an extraordinary assembly of shareholders.

Communism failed because the minority who realized the American dream through single party elections corrupted the majority, that is, by suppressing the holy trinity, the minority compensated for the forbidden American dream by paying for inactivity, and capitalism compensated for constant insecurity by exalting the spin to the sky that everyone has the chance to realize the American dream. Precisely that illusion, the only religion that does not gather people by means of the fear of punishment, but by means of rewards, is what holds the system together, all the parts of the mechanism of social reproduction.

5 THE AMERICAN DREAM, THE OFFICIAL RELIGION OF MANKIND

In cities it is not noticeable, there the churches are somehow too public, they are consumed by the fact that they are there for tourists, attractive, abundant, architectural, and it is not unimportant whether you go for coffee with your friends or to a family lunch after Mass. But, looking at churches in small towns, villages, it is easy to understand how necessary they are, it becomes clear that people need to be controlled, to be told a little bit about love and to be frightened a little from time to time, all those who shake the priests' hands after the service (as congratulations or thanks?) say, "Lovely sermon, reverend..." Looking at the little place, the rows of houses along the road and the little church, only big enough to hold the number of people who live in the village, it is easy to realize that this is *infrastructure*, television before television, it is easy to understand the exalted nature of the priestly vocation, that they in the end prevent us from killing each other with our bare hands and teeth. God's tears also help here, instead of lamps and fragrances, the ethereal fruit of the soul, which the masses usually call saints, reach the consciousness; it is irrelevant if they have been beatified. Their messages are not written down in black and white, but these moral characters communicate through the message of their life's work, on the screen of time, their own time, they walk the earth as tears roll down a face.

That is the base, this keeps us together, keeps the system stable. Some take part in stability because they love, or they lie successfully to themselves that they love, others because they are afraid, and that is enough for mankind to balance between immediate benefits and the fear of eternal damnation sufficiently well to increase productivity.

So… People choose politicians, they simply do not have a stronger weapon in their hands than elections, but they do not trust them, let's say, they choose the lesser evil. Peter's successors and priests are a form of comforter, meta-psychologists, but their power is limited because, in contrast to governments, they have no responsibility for the situation, and sin has accumulated over thousands of years, their reputation has fallen and with it their influence on the classes and the masses. So, when it is a matter of convincing the sisters and brothers that nothing is as valuable in this world as love, actually that love is the only reason for human existence, that education is necessary, that we need to go to war, or that the best choice in the world is to play football or start a group, the fulfilled American dreamers take the stage. Since the arrival of television, this work has been taken over by the successors of Peter's successors, and whenever the mass needs to be convinced of something, the fulfilled American dreamers take the stage.

Faith is not weak because Jesus has not been with us for more than two thousand years, nor would his descent amongst us strengthen it. The problem is human nature. A minor benefit today is still more valuable to billions than eternal life tomorrow, let alone wealth sufficient for lifelong abundant existence. It is not in human nature to believe in an event that happened several thousand years ago, nor to be satisfied with a reward after death. Rebellions against the management of the epoch, and church reforms, and everyday behaviour liberated from great words and acts, are proof that man needs instant benefit more than he fears punishment after death. That is why it is perfectly logical that the American dream should long ago have been declared the official religion of mankind.

It is easy to understand why it has not been. Because the vast majority of people are not fulfilled American dreamers, their need for comfort and *denial* has outvoted, silently overruled the logic of the matter. We live in a worldwide conspiracy of silence. Most people actively live out that conspiracy. That silence, that conspiracy have always existed, since man was defined by work, and woman by beauty, whereby man's definition by work does not reduce his and her requirement for him to be beautiful, nor does a woman's beauty free her from her and his desire for her to find realization on the labour market, or even better, to be owner of as much capital as possible.

Billions of marriages, a conspiracy of silence. People come before the priest, the registrar, or no one, and pledge eternal love, although there is no love, but, apart from the instinct to reproduce, only a conspiracy in which both are silent, and they marry one another either by law or by common-law, only because, due to their position within the law of supply and demand, they were not able to find anyone better.

Precisely this tendency of man to fool himself, most easily demonstrated by the billions of average or below average couples who pretend to be Julius Caesar and Cleopatra, and actually those billions are nothing other than divorce, domestic violence or in the best case a polite conspiracy of silence, compromise, fake – is also the key evidence that man will not accept anything less than the American dream in every way. It is not "fake it till you make it", but it's fake it; just fake it. Children, and adults too, on the meadow and tarmac, shout, "I am Ronaldo", "I am Rooney", adults say in silence, "I am Caesar," "I am Cleopatra", the acceptance of compromise is proof that man as a race does not accept anything less than the American dream.

Probably the American dream would have been proclaimed the official religion of mankind long ago, and then, freed from the ego chains of fear of failure, it would have advanced much more quickly, if, the problem suggests the solution, many had not tried to realize their American dream, and many did realize it, by collecting together inconsolable unfulfilled dreamers in a therapeutic conspiracy of silence.

Religion... in comparison with the number of people who believe, too few of them walk on water. Even in a poetic sense, not taking it literally, too few of them tear olive trees from the ground and cause mountains to dance.

Slaves, serfs, workers on a conveyor belt who wanted to be factory owners, fans, followers of pop stars, charity workers, all who ended up in the crowd instead of on the stage, and all who instead of in love ended up in fear, or with a wounded ego, looked for meta-psychologists/meta-psychiatrists, cried out for that therapy or comfort to be given an exalted name, and so numberless conspiracies of silence were born, that the only thing man as a race can accept is the realization of the American dream in every sense.

For some, others make that choice, most often parents, that is the land they are born in is chosen for them, but, like at a buffet, people choose religion as they choose a psychologist or psychiatrist, and also usually, like at a buffet, they take from religion what suits them. In the same way, like at a buffet, they choose whether Peter's successor or whoever's successor will be for them Michael Jordan, Roger Federer, Michael Jackson, Warren Buffet, Paul Krugman or Nikola Tesla.

We are born unfree and unequal. Equality is a thing that can never be attained, whereas freedom can be, for a small number.

It may be said that some people believe in God, and some say, think, they do not believe, they believe they do not believe. But while man chooses religion, he becomes a member of a religious community, he does not become an American dreamer, we are all born American dreamers.

In contrast to other ideologies, whose common characteristic is that people need to be persuaded to accept them, they do not believe in them, they do not doubt them, the American dream is written within a man like breathing or the instinct to propagate the species.

American dreamers are credible because their sermons are pure "how to" literature, completely aligned with human nature. American dreamers, in the service of maintaining any kind of social order, are the greatest and highest achievement of religious and political correctness known to man. They refer to the immediate past, and propagate a reward in this life.

For all these reasons it is clear, the only religion that unites the world is the American dream.

6 SHOW BUSINESS, THE SECT WITH THE LARGEST MEMBERSHIP

After all the initiatives to make the world a better place for everyone, and not just a good place for fulfilled American dreamers – which even God worked at and many whom God anointed – the world has not moved further than a crowd that is divided into the smallest group of owners of capital, a slightly larger group who spend their surplus value on culture, travel, various courses, visiting galleries and museums and so on, and the slightly frighteningly vast, vast majority of people who express themselves in one way or another through sport. If we extend the definition of sport to everything with rankings, we come to show business, showbiz.

"I would agree to live for all eternity in a place, where it has been established beyond doubt that it is impossible to undertake any form of exploit," wrote Venedikt Yerofeyev, which in liberal translation means that the peak of life is to die like a man, that is the same as being God, being God as far as your time, your epoch allows. But Earth is not a place where there is any corner where it has been established beyond doubt that it is impossible to undertake any form of exploit. Perhaps there are times like that in that place.

That is how it works.

In the beginning it is just life. Others bring the bread to the table, and you play with other children, make your clothes dirty and grow out of them, and this is enough for you to be called a human being. While you are young, if you do not lose what has been stupidly called virginity, it is absolutely certain that you lose in every possible way, you dream a little, and what makes you a man is the fact that no one understands you.

Later, you are just a man. To be a man still means that you eat when you are hungry and sleep when you are tired, but all of a sudden it is your job to worry about these things. Later it gets increasingly complicated, and comes down to the fact that you are a man if and only if *you own* both the territory on which and the time during which it is impossible to undertake an form of exploit. Alone or together in a group, you cannot avoid exploits, because man does not want anything more than to be God, to be *like God*, as close as possible to God, as like God as possible, the largest possible subset of God, that is a fulfilled American dreamer...

You cannot sell oil, you cannot expect that you will squeeze Shell or British Petroleum out of business, you will hardly push Bill Gates off the market, McDonald's has beaten most of its competition, Pret a Manger or Wrap Eat as well, so give up your attempt to construct a better car than Mercedes and the rest, General Motors holds the monopoly, give up any hope of beating Sony...

Studies of capital have clearly shown that, after the initial accumulation, and as a result the distribution of wealth and power, it is very rare for newly wealthy people to appear.

The vast majority of the newly rich have inherited their wealth, that is, their empire was left them by their ancestors. Some of them squander the inherited efforts of several generations, and someone else fills in the vacant spot, but the fact is that industry in the original meaning of the word, is not suitable ground for American dreamers. The enrichment of an individual by production is the rarest form of realization of the American dream.

In the world of multinational corporations, which occupied the land long ago, there is only room for visionaries who will offer the market something which does not exist at the moment, just as Frank McNamara thought up the credit card, Bill Gates offered an operating system, or Tim Berners-Lee the internet, and Mark Zuckerberg gave the passivization of the masses Facebook. In principle, an idea is required, the aim is to astound the market with something new, but, as far as the little man is concerned, almost all roads lead to showbiz.

Showbiz came about when the poor entertained the rich in the form of gladiators. At the very beginning of the biz slaves fought to the death in arenas, whether against each other or against starving animals.

The English lords organized boxing matches along the same lines. On the principle that the pay is proportionate to the number of people a man attracts to his activity, the fees were miserly, they consisted of small change and lunch, which was a slightly better salary than the daily wage for work in the fields or factory.

However, although the pay was poor, it was still pay, and Baron Pierre de Coubertin realized the potential of the entertainment industry in a flash, and put all his efforts into professional sport. Realizing that the hypocritical lords would outvote him, Coubertin was satisfied with the title of founder of the modern Olympic Games, but his basic notion was unstoppable.

With the growth in productivity/production, the middle classes appeared, and boxers and other modern gladiators no longer entertained only the rich, but the number of consumers of their product grew rapidly. Professional sport galloped towards its present day form, and was joined by showbiz as a whole.

The entertainment industry was born, which is the true dream factory. It is not just a factory of entertainment, but also of the American dream.

In contrast to the exact disciplines, science, applied science, in showbiz there is room for individuals, even self-taught individuals without any formal education, and sometimes it is sufficient to simply look good and know how to walk.

In the worship of idols an almost new religion was born, and the religion was, is and almost certainly always will be the idea that anyone can make it. And more than that! Everyone has an equal chance!

Capital helps God. When the axiom "God loves you" no longer has any effect, "capital loves you" takes the stage, and however much it doubts both of these, the collective consciousness will find it easier to believe that capital loves all people equally than that God loves everyone in the same way.

Actually, just as a child imitates his father, a grown man imitates God, that is he interprets him, behaves in a way that he thinks is imitating God, in short, man sees God either as an almighty tyrant or as a loving father. And life is a reaction to the level our dreams have been fulfilled. All human evils are nothing other than the reaction of the defeated to their failure to fulfil the American dream. Everything we read in the crime pages is nothing other than the defeated in the first round or the final of American dreaming smashing up the locker room. All the good in this world is only a visionary dreamer going to the garage from which he will attempt to conquer the world, like the Beatles or Steve Jobs, to the playing field where he will become Michael Jordan, to the agency that will make her Cindy Crawford, all the good is either going to the garage or the reaction of the winner, the Beatles, Steve Jobs, Jordan, Cindy... to their realization of the American dream.

People who can be happy and fulfilled, satisfied!, without realizing the American dream are so few, that it is hard to say whether their level of consciousness should be seen as exalted, or if it is in fact an illness, almost a deformity. The victorious minority is divided into the few humane ones who do not use their victory to suppress others simply because they can, and the rest.

The vast majority are unable to accept defeat. The defeated are angry, fury is the same thing as destruction, and we have already agreed that absolutely nothing should stand in the way of progress. In order to avoid smashing up the locker room, capital has shown everyone that it loves them equally, its penultimate argument for passivizing the masses is showbiz, and the final argument is the slogan that you do not have to be special at all to get so rich that you don't have to work any more. The lottery!

So, the American dream is a pillar of society because the desire to realize the American dream is so strong, that not only is it the perfect prevention of any excessive behaviour which might hinder progress, but as they protect their dreams, dreamers perform a large number of useful tasks. The greatest inventor of the world, Nikola Tesla, dug a canal, the rapper Eminem worked as a waiter, Rod Stewart was a gravedigger, Elton John entertained guests night after night in bars for a pound and a meal, and Madonna made porn. In the first phase they were ordinary hired workers fighting for freedom, and in the second they were the best advertisement for the fairness of the system, living proof that anyone is allowed to succeed, but he has to be persistent and capable.

A brother killed his brother because he was jealous, he was so jealous that not even the fear of God was enough to prevent the murder, but capital found a way to calm the defeated, or at least to neutralize them until they reach forty, after which they become biologically incapable of creating a storm at the shareholders' assembly; experts in managing the masses are not afraid of demonstrations in states where the average age of the population is forty. It is easy to govern a dead creature. You never give him what he wants, but lots of hope. And it is easy to govern the masses. From time to time you pull someone out of the mass and give him what they all want. People are born free and unequal. However much they resist reality with wishes, and however strong the wish for redemption from want is, the vast majority is perfectly aware that they do not possess the qualities necessary to realize the American dream. However, the system has taken care of that too: the owners of the means of production of the American dream regularly make the most ordinary mortals shamefully rich. Sometimes you activate the means for production of the American dream and you make someone dirty rich who is slightly better than the average. Madonna and Lady GaGa sing a little better than the average high school girl, they dance a little better, they are just a little bolder – and that is precisely the definition of pop, the performer must not be so good that he or she insults, demotivates the audience, precisely that is the foundation of the stability of this world, precisely because of the clearly very small difference between the fulfilled and the unfulfilled American dreamers, the American dream seems to be so damned attainable to the masses. The conviction that the chances are poor, but they still exist, the conviction that the conditions for realizing the American dream are received at birth, comforts even the most desperate. The common or garden lottery, the hope of winning money for a lavish, lifelong existence, is sufficient to get out of bed and pick up the remote control when you get home.

Indeed, are not more people tame because they believe they will get rich for life than because they believe in the Kingdom of Heaven?

7 CAPITAL IS THE BRIDGE TO GOD

Mankind is ready for an evolutionary leap, to throw off the excuses, the justifications for war, and communication of only the cause, the real reasons why war is waged. Simply, for a long time there has already been a critical mass of people for whom the explanation that a country was attacked because the government doesn't allow its people to watch television, or because the government of the attacked country does not respect the values of the attacking country, is either insulting or ridiculous. Also there has also long been a critical mass of sceptics who see a world government conspiracy or whatever in a chicken crossing the road. The predatory element is part of human nature, so all the conditions exist for the leader of a state to tell the voters very soon that they can either agree with an attack on a country to raze it to the ground, extract its natural wealth and/or give the destroyed country a bunch of loans, or they should not protest because they will lose the many privileges by which rulers corrupt their subjects. It is human nature to declare war, and the law of supply and demand will determine the price of a soldier. (It is important to point out that the routine organization of springs, summers or whatever season, in whichever territories, may not be communicated to the masses, because the admission that economic murderers exist would make the execution of the action more difficult, it would be more difficult to motivate the masses where this is necessary to realize their economic interests; the illusion of being part of the civilized progress of one's world view, if not sufficient, is still necessary.)

Human nature, which requires either the realization of the American dream or at least the largest possible part of the American dream as a whole, is seen to be literally comical, in the commotion, the negotiations by shareholders to hold an extraordinary shareholders' assembly, like Occupy Wall Street and the like (Stephane Hessel's "Rebel!" is one of the nicer comical ones, not even a speech at the shareholders assembly, but an invitation to the assembly). The masses of unfulfilled American dreamers, who attained their degree of neoliberalism in the store whilst choosing trousers or a telephone, produced by slave children, are evidence that man cannot accept anything less than the American dream and that the collective consciousness either has no free will, or it does not exist at all, but the acts of the collective consciousness are directed by capital, the only road from God through man back to God. Indeed, it is easier to choose a telephone or trousers politically correctly than to fear God's punishment, because they are of this world, but if you show the collective consciousness, which is uninformed, although that is impossible, that the trousers or the telephone were produced by a slave child and the image of a six-year old striker wailing whilst being beaten by an adult holding a truncheon, the collective consciousness will still buy the same trousers and the same telephone. We should not hold this against anyone, because this process is governed by capital, equally in moving production to China, equally in the construction of the first Chinese aircraft carrier, equally to the benefit of the banker who would be hanged by protester against globalisation, and to the benefit of the protester who would be hanged by the slave child because the protest of an unproductive importer is nothing other than the insistence that the policeman should beat the six-year-old exporter harder until his work becomes so expensive that the truncheon is held in his own hands.

Trousers or telephones not produced by child slaves may only be freely chosen by capital liberated from itself, that is, capital amassed so greatly in material and spiritual form that it becomes freedom (even if it is defined loosely as the absence of coercion, or compromise), the only field in which love grows. Capital wants man to become equal with God, for the collective consciousness capital is at the moment the only road that leads to God; refinement of the consciousness into freedom and love is nothing other than a function of productivity. It is absolutely clear that humanism will only win in circumstances in which humanism is in the interests of capital, just as it is perfectly clear that growth in productivity in the name of progress demands a growth in human rights, that is, humanism. God and capital want the same, for man to become equal to God, but on that path a camel will pass through the eye of a needle before an individual will enter the Kingdom of Heaven. But, as far as the collective consciousness is concerned, just as the ego dies only when it is well-fed, so the entrance of the collective consciousness into the Kingdom of Heaven is still a matter of productivity, which collects so much material and spiritual capital that it is set free, released from sin as it were. Capitalism, or the civil society, is the key evidence that enlightened dictatorship is the best form of government, in the constant search for an ideal ratio between state regulation and private enterprise. But several thousand years after man rejected God, his "independence", leaving home, it is completely clear that this enlightened dictator is capital.

Aware that people are born unfree and unequal, that is, only equal in the desire to realize the American dream, understanding that the realization of the American dream is the privilege of the most capable or at least the most fortunate minority, we American dreamers, in the name of the progress of both the collective consciousness and the individual, give up all forms of protection, apart from those arising out of the trinity of capital, the law of supply and demand and American dreaming.

As Peter the Great put it, you have to rule or you have to be ruled. He was a great admirer of Isaac Newton, so he often said that a force can be neutralized by the same force, but overcome by a stronger one. The force with which an organized minority governs the unorganized majority is emotion, a derivative of the ego.

Behaviourists know that you can persuade a man to go to war by selling ego, even if that means a barehanded charge against a tank, so why then would you not be able – if you don't sell clothes or telephones, but lifestyle – to persuade him to spend money he does not have on things he does not need in order to impress people he does not care about?! All this to be someone, to be something, so that, if he can't have enough wealth to live the rest of his life in abundance, he can earn, buy, steal, take as much as he can, and at least live a tiny piece of the American dream. But, true freedom, and with it love, begins where even the realization of the American dream is not enough, where the power of money ends, and *not enough!* redefines man.

We American dreamers do not get carried away. We know that democracy is founded on people who rejoice if a penalty is awarded to their team for a foul, which happened, or even did not happen, twenty metres from the goal and in those circumstances, every protest is in fact a protest against our own genes or the number on the dice.

If God came down amongst people, performed a few tricks to show that he really is God, and make an ideal distribution of resources on Earth for the whole of mankind, and those resources were enough for one hundred thousand years, a group would appear which would want to take them over, simply to spite the rest, to enjoy their suffering; that is human nature.

The American dream is rebellion against the reality that resists our desires, rebellion happens as a reaction to want, and it begins "in the garage".

The American dream is an individual revolution which results in an equal number of casualties as a mass armed one, but their sacrifices are smaller, they are in the end invested and not spent lives.

American dreaming is not a struggle for the common good, it is a purely individual matter, and it is manifest as association in small groups, however the efforts of individuals to get so rich that they no longer have to work in history have resulted in greater benefit for the masses than so-called movements for equality and the betterment of the masses.

The American dream is the highest level of collective consciousness.

May the owners of the means of production of the American dream, but also the owners of other means of production, rejoice in the unnumbered army of American dreamers! For, what can an American dreamer lose except his mediocrity, and he may gain abundance for the rest of his life!

American dreamers, you are useful! And that is no small thing.

American Dreamers of all Countries, you're all alone!

Tomislav Birtic
Manifesto of American Dreamers

Publisher
Tomislav Birtic

Translation
Janet Ann Tuskan

Design
Zarko Kuvalja

Title page photograph
Dreamstime.com / Bejhan Jusufi

ISBN-10: 1468182684
ISBN-13: 978-1468182682

44